Spirit of the
WOLF

Spirit of the
WOLF

Mythical Hunter of the Wilderness

Bath • New York • Cologne • Melbourne • Delhi
Hong Kong • Shenzhen • Singapore

This edition published by Parragon Books Ltd in 2017 and distributed by

Parragon Inc.
440 Park Avenue South, 13th Floor
New York, NY 10016
www.parragon.com

Designed, produced, and packaged by
Stonecastle Graphics Limited

Text and captions by Shaun Ellis
Photographs © Monty Sloan
Edited by Maggie Lofts
Designed by Sue Pressley and Paul Turner
Cover designed by Shona Cutt

ISBN 978-1-4748-8685-7

Printed in China

CONTENTS

KINDRED SPIRITS

I grew up in a farming community where there were few other children, and so I made friends with the wildlife in the surrounding countryside. I felt at home in woodland at night, and I learned to use my senses of smell and hearing to find my way around. I bonded with the badgers and foxes who were fearless and relaxed in my presence. For many years, I was privileged to be able to watch their family groups and study their behavior.

So how did a young man from rural England end up at the foot of the Rocky Mountains in Idaho studying wolves under the guidance of the Nez Perce Native Americans? It was mostly due to hard work, perseverance and a chance encounter with a Native American biologist at a wolf seminar, who I persuaded to take me on as a volunteer. Working with him and fellow students by day, and studying the wolves on my own by night, I slowly earned the respect of the amazing Nez Perce people.

It was here in two to three feet of snow that I realized the best way to learn about wolves was to return to the ways of my childhood and live alongside them. And a few years later, I decided to try to join a wild pack not as a leader but as a low-ranking member, because I understood that only in this position would the wolves be prepared to teach me about their society.

I now work with captive wolves at Wolf Pack Management, Combe Martin, Devon, England and through the in-depth study of their behavior, my colleagues and I are constantly discovering new sides to these fascinating animals. I hope that I can use this knowledge to help protect wolves for future generations to study and admire.

Shaun Ellis
AUTHOR

WOLVES IN FOCUS

Though I studied geology at university, wolves soon took over from rocks as a source of inspiration, and I started to focus on these fascinating animals. An interest in photography grew into a career: I have been taking pictures of wolves in color and black and white since 1984 and have accumulated an extensive library of wolf images.

Despite decades of research, both in captivity and in the field; despite success in recovery programs in the upper Midwest and Northern Rockies; despite growing public support for wolves and predators in general; despite the fact that you are far more likely to be killed by a toaster than a wild predator, especially a wolf; this animal remains in peril, or has already become locally extinct in many parts of the world.

So since 1988 to help conserve and promote the wolf, I have been working as a handler, lecturer, researcher, and photographer at Wolf Park in Indiana, USA. Wolf Park is home to several packs of gray wolves, and part of the proceeds from my photographic sales go to the park to support education initiatives. Working with captive wolves has allowed me to get really close to my subjects, and I've been able to capture intimate behavior that would have been extremely difficult to shoot in the wild. I also design and maintain various websites, most of which are dedicated to wolf conservation.

Field studies, especially those conducted in Yellowstone National Park, have shown the importance of the wolf as a key species in the ecosystem – yet the wolf still remains a maligned, feared, and misunderstood predator. I can only hope that we can now come to accept the wolf for what it is, rather than live in fear for what it is not.

Monty Sloan
PHOTOGRAPHER

SPIRIT OF THE WOLF

Throughout history, wolves have been a constant source of fascination to humans as well as awakening some of our deepest fears. Featured in myths, legends, fables, and folklore, the relationship between humans and wolves is both ancient and complex. From the unsettling children's bedtime story *Little Red Riding Hood* to frightening tales of humans becoming werewolves when the moon is full, we are familiar with the traditional image of the wolf as both a cunning predator and an evil supernatural monster, but is there any truth in these popular myths?

And what of the gentler side of the wolf's nature? Tales of lost children being raised by wolves exist in many cultures, and these ancient stories, together with more recent ones, such as Rudyard Kipling's *The Jungle Book*, suggest that wolves possess superior parental skills. In fact, today the parenting skills of wolves are highly respected by zoologists and animal behaviorists

who consider that, within the entire animal kingdom, only humans and some other primates can equal the care and education they offer to their young.

One of the earliest and best known legends of wolves and human children is the fourth-century story of the Roman twins Romulus and Remus. These sons of Mars and Rhea Silvia, a vestal virgin, were thrown into the River Tiber in a basket by Amulius, who saw them as a threat to his rule of Alba Longa. When they floated ashore, a "she-wolf" heard their cries and suckled them. After being found and brought up by a royal shepherd, the twins later became the founders of Rome.

Wolf mythology is filled with stories about wolves raising orphaned or lost children, and these tales represent a positive attitude toward the wolf and its relationship with human society. Sadly, however, myths also portray the wolf in a negative light, helping to create a climate of fear among the people of Europe, in

particular, who throughout history have set about hunting the wolf almost to extinction.

For example, the legendary beast of Gévaudan, said to be a giant wolf, reportedly killed about 100 people, over a three-year period, in the Auvergne region of France in the mid-eighteenth century. Such was its ferocity that King Louis XV called out his troops to hunt it down. Even though a large wolf was killed, the attacks continued until two more wolves were slaughtered, both of which were thought to be the beast.

The wolf's association with evil is still fueled today by horror movies, which portray wolf-like creatures transformed by a full moon and driven by a thirst for human blood. So this insatiable interest in the wolf's traditional reputation as a fierce killer continues today. Interestingly, a recent survey, which sought children's attitudes toward the wolf, highlighted that more young people are afraid of the wolf's howl than of the animal itself, which has become familiar to them through modern documentary television programs and natural history books.

In fact, proven attacks by a healthy wild wolf on people are almost non-existent. Wolves that act aggressively toward humans are usually suffering from an illness, such as rabies, and in captivity, attacks are more likely to occur if animals have been poorly handled by their keepers.

Native American legends tell of a sacred pact between wolves and humans to respect each other's families and land. Arguably, the wolf has honored its side of the agreement, but, sadly, we have not, instead we have systematically eradicated the wolf from much of its former habitat.

Today, the dedicated work of conservationists and animal behaviorists has helped us to understand the nature of the wolf and its vital role in the natural world. As ever more wilderness is destroyed due to increased

development and the destruction of natural habitat, nature reserves have allowed the wolf to survive in areas where its very existence was gravely threatened.

This book offers us the privileged opportunity to learn about the secret world of the wolf through the eyes of Shaun Ellis, who was shown the mystical ways of the

wolf by the Nez Perce Native Americans, and who has lived with wolves and studied them for many years.

With stunning photography by Monty Sloan, whose unique viewpoint enables us to glimpse the fascinating world of the wolf from within the pack, this book offers a remarkable insight into the spirit of the wolf.

Natural balance

Top predators, such as the wolf, help to maintain a balanced environment. In wooded areas, deer kill trees by stripping and eating bark, and so by controlling deer numbers, wolves help conserve trees, which are an essential habitat for birds and other wildlife.

White Protector
According to Native American legend, if a white wolf is seen either in a dream or reality, it has been sent to protect you. The Native Americans respected the wolf's strong family values, among other qualities.

On the brink
Wild wolves live on the brink of starvation for most of their lives, but the adult wolves always return with food for their pups, realizing the importance of the next generation in increasing pack numbers and ensuring hunting success.

The parenting skills of wolves are highly respected by zoologists and animal behaviorists who consider that, within the entire animal kingdom, only humans and some other primates can equal the care and education they offer to their young.

Pup school
Young wolves receiving lessons in life from their nanny. The nanny is selected by the alpha female before the birth of her pups to continue their care and education once they are weaned at four to six weeks of age. This enables the alpha female to devote herself once more to leading her pack.

Dangerous game

There is a constant risk of injury for wolves when hunting large quarry. A kick from a bison or a stab from a deer stag's antlers could be fatal. Adult wolves use the antlers and legs of dead prey during play to teach the young wolves avoidance techniques.

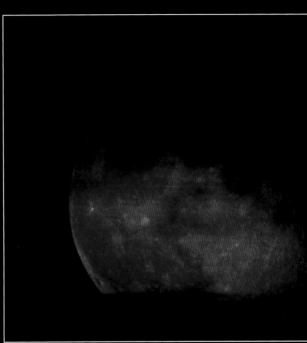

The stuff of myth
Images such as this, with a wolf howling at a full moon, have
fueled the human imagination, and horror stories often portray
the wolf as a vicious killer with a taste for human blood.

A recent survey, which sought

children's attitudes toward the wolf,

highlighted that more young people are

afraid of the wolf's howl than of

the animal itself.

WOLF MYTHOLOGY

From the northern Rockies of North America to the Carpathian Mountains in Europe, wherever there were wolves, human societies have surrounded them with folklore and superstitions, some of which have led to the demise of the wolf in many areas. Other cultures, however, such as Native American ones, have revered wolves and granted them an almost God-like status.

NATIVE AMERICAN CULTURE

One Native American tribe – the Shoshone – believed that coyotes and wolves had created the world and that after death the spirit of a tribal member was taken to the land of the coyote. The wolf guarded the path walked by the dead, and it would first awaken and then wash a human soul in the river. The newly cleaned spirit could then gain entry into the Promised Land.

As human populations increased, wolves began to seek sanctuary in the remote mountainous regions. As a result, Native Americans bestowed even greater mystic importance on the wolf, and they studied the animal in an effort better to understand it and learn from its wisdom. They say that the wolf taught them about co-operation for living together in extended families, and they learned the importance of social structure – they respected their chieftains in the same way that wolves respect the decision-making role of alphas.

Because of its ability to discover new places and find its way around its huge territory, the wolf became known as The Pathfinder. Native hunters often found elk and bison by following the wolves, whose sharp senses of smell and hearing enabled them to detect prey long before their human counterparts. The Native hunters never killed without leaving some meat as a thank you for their wolf helpers. The Native American tribes of the Great Plains believed that they could become great warriors by observing the wolf's hunting

20

skills. The sign for the Pawnee, one of the most feared tribes on the plains, was the same as the sign for wolf. And the Lakota tribes respected and honored the wolf's loyalty to its mate and family, and before hunting they would smear red dye on their mouths to mimic a feeding wolf.

The Native Americans and the wolf had a pact to support each other, but when Europeans began to colonize North America huge numbers of wolves were killed. Many tribes felt that the pact had been broken, and the Blackfoot and Lakota believed that a gun used to kill a wolf would never shoot straight again.

Native Americans have many stories that tell of shape-shifting: the ability to change from human to a different animal form. According to one old legend, a Native American woman found a wolf pup while out collecting wood for her tribe. The animal was alone, starving and close to death. She carried the wolf back to her camp where she fed him and kept him warm in her tepee. He grew quickly and they became inseparable friends. One morning they went to the river to drink, and in the soft mud the woman saw their tracks from the previous evening; human and wolf footprints turned into two sets of wolf tracks. Confused by what she saw, the woman sought advice from the old chief who told her that as recompense for the tiny life she had saved the wolf had given her the gift of existing in two forms: human and wolf. That evening she sat by the water with her wolf companion and looked at her reflection, and a female wolf looked back at her.

Spiritual cleaner

The wolf's natural love of water inspired some Native American folklore. The wolf was believed to guard the path walked by the dead, where it would wash the human soul in water before the newly cleaned spirit gained entry to the Promised Land.

EUROPEAN CULTURE

The wolf has for centuries captured the imagination of different cultures and features strongly in the complex body of European folklore and mythology. Several of Aesop's fables (c.600 BC) refer to the wolf's cunning; "The Boy Who Cried Wolf" is one of the best known. After the shepherd boy had sounded many false alarms, his cries of "A wolf!" are ignored by the townspeople. To the boy's dismay, his sheep are attacked by wolves and he is left helpless. Similarly, *Little Red Riding Hood*, a children's fairy story which originated in the seventeenth century, reinforces this perception of the wolf as a cunning predator.

Not only are there such stories of wolves dressing up as humans, but there are also ones in which humans turn into wolves. A number of cultures have "were" creatures, often inspired by the most dangerous animal found in the area. There were "were-tigers" in India, "were-leopards" in Africa, and "were-wolves" in medieval Europe. The term "were" is taken from the old English word "wer," meaning "man," thus werewolves or man-wolves were believed to be half-human and half-wolf.

Humans who became werewolves of their own free will were supposed to have made a pact with the devil. Most werewolf transformations took place at night when the moon was full; the werewolf attacked, killed and often ate people and animals, returning to human form at daybreak. On the other hand, people could sometimes inherit the condition. In Greece, for instance, anyone suffering from epilepsy was thought to be a werewolf.

There are various possible explanations for the origin of werewolf myths. A person living in one of the vast European forests 700 to 800 years ago could very easily have been mistaken for a wolf or werewolf. Receding and bleeding gums, sometimes coupled with excessive hair growth, are signs of severe malnutrition, which

would have been common at that time among the poor. Village outcasts trying to scavenge a living might have moved like wolves or mimicked their hunting behavior in an effort to feed themselves. And the wearing of animal skins – often wolfskins because of their outstanding insulating qualities – afforded protection from the cold. Another theory suggests that the poor conditions in which grain was stored at the time might have led to a variety of hallucinogenic

Safe routes
Wolves often use well-worn paths when moving around their territories. With daily scent-marking, these paths become safe areas where attacks from rival packs are unlikely.

reactions. So perhaps something as ordinary as a slice of bread, which might have contained bad rye seed, could have induced a werewolf sighting.

Today we also recognize the existence of a condition known as lycanthropy, which is a form of schizophrenia during which a patient believes that he or she is a wild animal, often a wolf or a werewolf. Sufferers have been observed making growling and snarling noises and chewing on furniture as if it were prey. In other non-European countries, characteristics of similarly powerful beasts common to the region, such as tigers in India, for example, are displayed by patients.

One of the most famous wolf stories is that of St Francis and the wolf of Gubbio, which can be found in *The Little Flowers of St Francis*, an anonymous fourteenth-century source of St Francis stories. The story tells of how St Francis tamed a large wolf that was terrorizing the good people of Gubbio, a town in

Under cover of darkness

The wolf's nocturnal habits added to its mystery, fueling numerous legends and horror stories. The wolf is, in fact, an intelligent, shy animal that avoids interaction with humans.

Umbria, Italy. While St Francis was staying in the town he was told of a wolf that had become so ravenous that it was not only killing and eating their livestock but also people.

The inhabitants of Gubbio became afraid to go outside the town walls, and so St Francis took pity not only on the people but on the wolf, too, and decided to go out and meet the animal. The townspeople desperately tried to warn St Francis of the danger, but he insisted that God would protect him. One brave friar and several peasants accompanied him outside the town gates, but soon after leaving, the peasants became terrified and refused to go any further. St Francis and the friar walked on, and suddenly the wolf charged at them from the forest, its jaws wide open. St Francis made the sign of the cross at the wolf and it immediately slowed down, and closed its mouth. St Francis then called out

to the wolf: "Come to me Brother Wolf, I wish you no harm," and at once the wolf lowered its head and laid down at the feet of St Francis. He asked why the wolf had been killing the people of Gubbio and their animals. "Brother Wolf", said St Francis, "I would like you to make peace with the townspeople, they will harm you no more and you must no longer harm them, all your past wrongs will be forgiven."

The wolf displayed its agreement by moving its body and nodding its head. In front of the crowd that had gathered, St Francis asked the wolf to make a pledge. He extended his hand and the wolf in turn extended its paw to seal the peace pact. St Francis then invited the wolf to follow him into the town. By the time they reached the square, everyone had gathered to witness the miracle. He then offered the townspeople peace on behalf of the wolf. The townsfolk promised to feed the animal, and St Francis asked the wolf if it could live under these terms. The wolf lowered its head and twisted its body in agreement. This convinced everyone that the wolf was willing to accept the pact. The animal once more placed its paw in St Francis's hand.

From that day the wolf and the townspeople kept their pact. The wolf went from house to house and was given food. When it finally died of old age, the people of Gubbio were sad. The wolf's peaceful ways had been a constant reminder to them of the tolerance and holiness of St Francis, and they had seen it as a living symbol of the providence of God. St Francis had educated them to accept the wolf and, in return, the wolf had accepted them.

Native respect

The Native Americans respected all animals and believed that each one had special qualities and skills that they could learn from: none more so than the bison and the wolf.

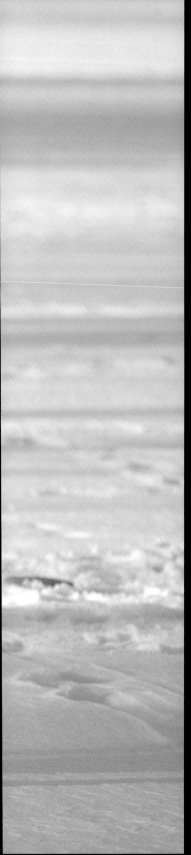

The wolf has for centuries captured the imagination of different cultures and features strongly in the complex body of European folklore and mythology.

Relative differences
European wolves (above) are generally smaller than their North American counterparts (left), and tend to be shorter, darker and more thickly set.

Wherever there were wolves, human societies have surrounded them with folklore and superstitions.

Bedtime stories
Children's fairy stories, such as *Little Red Riding Hood,* which originated in Europe in the seventeenth century, reinforced the perception of the wolf as a cunning predator.

THE PACK

Wolves originated in the New World about five million years ago. During the Pleistocene epoch (the last ice age), the dire wolf was the largest known species of wolf ever to exist. But it was a much smaller species that crossed into Siberia from Alaska, and this species eventually developed into the larger gray wolf *Canis lupus* of today. It settled in Eurasia and also migrated back to North America where it populated much of what is now known as Canada and the United States, except for one small region in the south-eastern US, which was home to a smaller wolf known as the red wolf *Canis rufus*.

Thanks to many detailed studies by biologists in the wild, we now know much more about the behavior of gray wolves, including the complex ways they use sound, smell, and posture, which are all specific to a particular rank, to communicate with each other.

The close-knit pack, usually consisting of eight to 12 animals, comprises a pair of high-ranking individuals known as the alpha male and alpha female. These two animals lead the pack but, contrary to previous supposition, are not always the largest wolves. They make all the necessary decisions to protect the pack and its territory, and in return they are usually the only two animals that will breed.

VISUAL COMMUNICATION

The muzzle is one of the most important parts of the wolf's body for communication and to kill prey. The alpha male and female are usually easy to recognize within the family because, among other characteristics, their muzzles are clearly highlighted with bold lines and colors, which act as a clear visual deterrent to members of other packs who will instantly register their status.

It is often said that a direct stare into a wolf's or dog's eyes represents a challenge. But rather than our eyes, it

now seems that it is more likely to be our teeth that convey dominance. Adult wolves teach pups to avert their muzzles when approaching adults in the pack by snapping into the air near the pups' heads to make them turn or lower their heads. Having learned this at an early age, adult wolves lower their heads as a mark of respect to a more dominant pack member.

The head position adopted by each animal depends on its position within the social order. For example, a mid- to high-ranking animal would show respect to a higher family member by moving its muzzle horizontally to either the right or left. If respect is not shown, the dominant animal is entitled to move its own muzzle to either the right or left of the offender's muzzle. This intimidation is usually all that is needed to gain a demonstration of respect, but if more pressure is required, the higher-ranked animal will issue a low, throaty growl, with increasing intensity if necessary, backed up by facial expressions. A snap into the air just to the side of the muzzle will be the final warning before the use of physical force.

The wolf's ear positions also play a vital role in communication. They can be splayed sideways (resembling outstretched wings) to indicate defence, or extended and pointed forward to gain respect by drawing attention to the muzzle.

The hackles are sometimes raised around the neck and shoulders to give the impression of increased size during defensive situations. A dominant animal has a continuous bold line that extends from the neck all the way along the spine to the tip of the tail, the bolder and more continuous the line, the higher the rank of the animal.

One as yet unproven theory among biologists is that the different types of food eaten by the specific ranks within the pack affect their color and markings as well as their scent patterns. An ageing alpha will be demoted when there is a suitable younger candidate in the pack,

and the older animal will no longer be able to consume the best parts of the kill. Photographic evidence has recorded a change in the markings and color of demoted individuals sometime after this, suggesting direct links between food, markings and rank.

SCENT-MARKING

The dominant alpha male and female are recognized just as easily by their smell as by their appearance. As the highest-ranking wolves, they will consume the best quality food from each kill: essential organs, such as heart, liver, kidneys, and the best fresh meat, along with possibly the brain, which will give them a stronger smell than any other pack member. Each rank within the pack is allowed to consume a different part of the carcass, ensuring that each emits a different scent.

The strong scent of the alpha pair is essential for defending the pack's territory as rival packs will avoid trespassing into another pack's territory only if the invisible scent barrier is strong and powerful. The alphas will lay scent down in a variety of different patterns – by urinating, defecating and rubbing around trees on the borders of their territory – designed to send different messages either to rival packs or to lone wolves operating within the buffer zones between established families. Raised-leg urination is used only by the alpha wolves as this enables them to spray their strong-smelling urine to a much higher level on trees and bushes, which is essential for marking and defending their territory.

Seasonal changes affect the variety and intensity of scent patterns, continually altering the level of potential threat from neighboring packs. It is the responsibility of the dominant male, as the protector of his family, to maintain and reinforce the scent patterns that define their territory, and it is vital for this purpose that he consumes the best parts from each kill.

Leader of the pack

This alpha wolf can be identified by both its posture and bold coat markings – note the difference in color to the wolf on the left. Alphas are not always the biggest and boldest animals in the pack, but they do have a piercing stare and bold attitude.

A snap into the air just to the side of the muzzle will be the final warning before the use of physical force.

VOCAL COMMUNICATION

Growls, yips, yaps, and whines are vocalisations used at close range in combination with body language. The howl is a long-range method of communicating with pack members who are out of sight, or with rival wolves, in which case it is used as a way of avoiding conflict and can be heard several miles away. Each animal has a different sound depending on its pack status. The alpha pair's howl is low in tone, and they can also be identified by the length of the pauses between howls. It may not be the alpha wolves which initiate the howling, but they will quickly assume control of the situation once vocal contact is made with, for example, a neighboring pack, a lone wolf, or a family member that has become lost while hunting. If the alpha wolves consider that the pack needs to prolong its calls, they will offer encouragement to howl by repeating a long, deep howl or if they want to stop the pack, a series of two or three cut-off howls in quick succession.

THE BETAS

Second in rank to the alpha pair are the betas, which are also usually a pair of animals, where numbers permit, which hold disciplinary positions within the family. Betas are easy to recognize because they are often the biggest and boldest animals in the pack; they rely on their strength to establish pack rules passed down by the alpha pair. The beta's role is that of enforcer, deflecting much of the potential danger away from the valuable alphas. Their spine markings, though quite bold, are broken, in contrast to the strong and continuous lines of the alphas.

The betas are vocally quite low in tone: not as low as the alphas but lower than the remaining pack members. They howl for approximately three to four times longer than the alphas, adding strength and continuity to the pack calls.

Top marks

An alpha wolf can also be recognized by its bold facial markings, in particular on the muzzle, ears, and around the eyes, which distinguish it from the other wolves. It will also have a very strong scent.

Alpha line

The alpha's hackles have a bold outline, and a dark line continues down the body, creating the outline of a saddle on its back, and runs right to the base of the tail.

THE LOWER RANKS

Lower in rank than the betas is a group known as the mid-ranking wolves, which are usually led by a pair of more dominant wolves: the female teaches and disciplines subordinate females and the male performs the same role with the male wolves. These animals receive information from the alpha pair via the betas. In large packs of wolves with up to 15 animals, this line of communication is vital in order for the alpha pair to retain control.

The main duty of the mid-ranking wolves is to create the illusion that there are more wolves in the pack than there actually are. This is done in several ways and helps the pack defend its territory. The mid-ranking wolves vary their diet so that their scent-markings never remain the same, thus giving the illusion of a larger number of wolves. And during howling, the mid-ranking wolves use a variety of sounds – yips, yaps, barks, whines, howls, and growls – to make it hard for packs in neighboring territories to identify exactly how many wolves are in the pack. Mid-ranking wolves are naturally suspicious and are always aware of anything new or unfamiliar. The alpha and beta wolves rely on them to alert the pack to any danger.

The pack is completed by the specialists: the hunters, the nannies and the much misunderstood omega wolves. Hunters are often female as they are 20-25 percent smaller than the males and therefore much faster. This gives them the ability to catch the prey or cut off the escape route of the intended quarry. But males

A dominant animal has a continuous bold line that extends from the neck all the way along the spine to the tip of the tail, the bolder and more continuous the line, the higher the rank of the animal.

Under exposure

This wolf (opposite) is showing respect by exposing its light underside. It is also showing that it trusts the dominant animal because it has exposed the most vulnerable parts of its body; a single bite to these areas could kill.

Marks of respect

An alpha wolf's bold outlines can be seen from some distance and are used in conjunction with body posture, scent, and sound to gain respect from fellow or rival pack members.

Alpha and beta

The bold markings of the alpha wolf (left) clearly distinguish it from the beta wolf on the right.

Strong second

The beta wolves (opposite) are the biggest and boldest wolves in the pack. They are responsible for enforcing the wishes of the alpha pair and are sent forward to do a recce in times of danger.

are also required for their strength, particularly when hunting large prey such as bison. The female hunter may separate the quarry from the herd and tire it, but she would need the assistance of the larger male hunter to pull the animal down.

Nannies are specialist female or male wolves selected by the alpha female to care for and educate her pups once they are weaned, when she returns to her duties as leader of the pack.

Omega wolves are essential to the survival of the wolf pack. They are responsible for defusing tension within the pack and minimizing injury. From the age of two to three weeks, the omega pup is always at the center of constant bouts of quarreling among its litter-

mates. The omega learns very quickly how to attract attention toward itself by playing games and acting like a "court jester" or clown. Then by using a series of instinctive and learned behaviors, ranging from body postures, facial expressions, and vocal sounds, the omega is able to calm a situation, avoid injury, and restore harmony.

The omega wolf has often been labeled as the "Cinderella wolf" because it was assumed to be low-ranking and mistreated. This could be because when a wolf pack is feeding, the omega has been seen to be chased away, often repeatedly, from the carcass. One possible explanation for this behavior is to allow the high-ranking animals to change position at the carcass

without fighting. This ensures that they get the select parts and the right amount of food for their rank. Hungry wolves could seriously injure each other without the distraction provided by the omega. Once the other wolves have fed, the omega is rewarded by being allowed access to some high-quality food that has been saved for it specifically by a beta wolf. So it is probable that, despite appearances, the omega holds a high-ranking specialist position which is valued within the pack.

The omega howl is the most tuneful in the pack, reaching both high and low notes, and by bringing harmony to a bout of howling, it can help to calm the pack when it is on the defensive.

The main duty of the mid-ranking wolves is

Remaining flexible

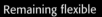

The mid-ranking animals have quite neutral markings, which allow them to change their rank if necessary. When a wolf dies, they may be required to fill a high-ranking or a specialist position.

Pack hierarchy

These pictures show how a low-ranking wolf is expected to turn its muzzle away when a dominant member of the pack approaches. If it fails to do this, the dominant wolf will resort to "mouthing" on the muzzle or neck areas to command respect.

The strong scent of the alpha pair is essential for defending the pack's territory.

Staying high

Scent-rolling helps to maintain a high position in the pack. Fish is often used because of its strong smell. The wolf rolls on the fish and rubs its scent onto its nose, head, back, and tail.

Bonding sessions

Close family bonds are reinforced by frequent rubbing of scent against pack members. Other bonding activities include grooming and play.

Rival packs will avoid trespassing into another pack's territory

only if the invisible scent barrier is strong and powerful.

Membership application

A lone wolf howls frequently to gain information from surrounding packs. It can tell if a rank is absent from the response and can then decide whether to try to enroll.

Howling from on high

Wolves often prefer to howl from an elevated position in order to project the sound further. They can also be seen standing in a semicircle during howling to project their sound in different directions.

Alpha duet

A breeding alpha pair often indicates their breeding rights by howling. When the alpha female comes into season, there will be visible spots of blood in her urine. By urinating over it, the alpha male is proclaiming his right to mate with her.

Sound disguise

The wolf pack howls for a variety of reasons including defence. It relies on the mid-ranking animals vocally to create the illusion that there are many more individuals within the pack.

The howl is a way of communicating with pack members close by or out of sight, or with rival wolves, in which case it is used as a way of avoiding conflict.

Howling lessons
Communication through howling is taught to the young wolves at an early age, and they are rewarded with food and praise. Each pup learns the howl relevant to its own rank.

Vocal flare

A wolf away from its pack will often call them using a rallying or locating howl. This wolf doesn't expect to get a reply but is just sending out a vocal beacon so the pack can find him or her again.

Low equals high

The alpha howl is low in tone which is a sign of its high status in the pack. It howls for short periods and then stops to listen to any response so he or she can decide whether the pack as a whole should continue or stop.

Wolf gazing

The wolf's eyesight is poor in comparison to its other senses. Its lingering stare has often been likened to a human gaze and was said to be why the Native Americans referred to the animal as

Sensitive hearing

Wolves can hear rival packs up to 10 miles away on open ground. The mid-ranking animals are naturally suspicious and often hear things before the rest of the pack, alerting them to

Pack jesters

Omega wolves were once wrongly thought to be the lowest ranking in the pack, but they are, in fact, highly respected and allowed to feed on good-quality meat as their reward for defusing tension in volatile situations, such as during feeding.

By using a series of instinctive and learned behaviors, ranging

from body postures, facial expressions, and vocal sounds, the omega

is able to calm a situation, avoid injury, and restore harmony.

Omega wolves are essential to the survival of the wolf pack. They are responsible for defusing tension within the pack and minimizing injury.

Peace-keepers

An omega wolf (right) uses its posture and vocal tones to
calm a hostile situation. This is a vital role in all wolf packs.

Meet and greet
After time apart, pack bonds are re-established with licking and tail wagging. This behavior
has also been seen when family members that have joined other packs meet up again.

Means of communication

Body postures make up a large percentage of the wolf's communication at short distance, and this is reinforced with facial expressions, ear and tail positions, use of hackles, and vocal sounds.

Thanks to many detailed studies by biologists in the wild, we now know much more about the behavior of wolves, including the complex ways they use sound, smell, and posture, which are all specific to a particular rank, to communicate with each other.

Size constraints

A wolf's territory can range from just a few to several hundred miles. This, together with the availability of food, determines the size of the pack.

75

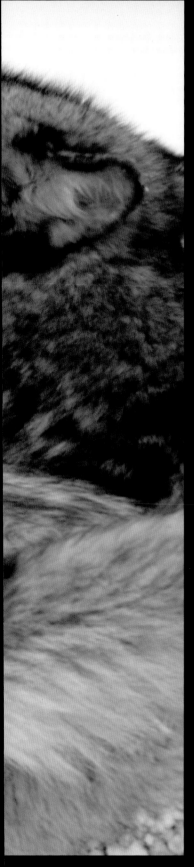

The Magnificent Seven
A wolf pack varies in size from as few as three to twenty animals. Generally, a pack consists of the alpha pair and their young, betas, mid-ranking wolves, and the specialists, such as the omegas.

Wisdom of age
In most wolf packs there are ageing animals that are valued for their knowledge and life experience, like grandparents in human society. These wolves are often selected as nannies and take part in educating and teaching the pups.

*The head position adopted by each
animal depends on its position within
the social order.*

Variety packs
Pack size depends on the amount of available habitat and how many wolves are needed
to defend and hunt within it. European packs (above) now usually occupy small territories
unlike North American wolves (right), which inhabit vast areas of open plains and forest.

Cleaning contract
It is the right of an alpha to both groom and be groomed by other pack members. Grooming helps the pack to bond and removes dirt and parasites from their fur.

Dual-purpose coat

During winter, the wolf develops a thick fur coat (right) to keep it warm. This is divided into two layers: the top layer of fur, called guard hair, keeps the animal dry in snow and rain, and the layer of soft fur underneath keeps it warm. The thick winter coat is molted in the spring months ready for warmer summer temperatures (above).

Winter warmers

During the winter, wolves always appear much larger as they have developed their thick, thermal winter coats, which help them survive in harsh weather conditions and low temperatures.

Wolf's clothing

The varied coloration and markings on the wolf's coat allow it to blend into its natural surroundings. Camouflage is vital for hiding from both predator and prey.

No wolf's land

A lone wolf passing through a strange territory will often urinate in water to remain undetected. This wolf has no territory of its own but operates in the buffer zone, a neutral area between existing packs where it is usually safe to travel.

Smelly feet

Wolves can strengthen territorial boundaries by means of scent glands in their feet. A beta wolf will also leave scratch-marks as a visual deterrent along with its scent

Liquid asset

A wolf pack's territory will usually contain a water source, ranging from lakes to streams.

Wolves need large quantities of water after feeding and during pregnancy.

Natural swimmers

Wolves, with their large feet and long legs, are good swimmers, and they can easily cross lakes and rivers in their territory. Though they catch and eat fish in shallow water, they rarely follow large prey into water.

Fleet of foot

Hunters are specialist animals and tend to be smaller and quicker than other pack members. They therefore tend to be females, but the strength of the males will also be needed to help bring down large prey.

Speed merchants

The maximum speed that a
wolf can run is between 30
and 40mph, and this can be
maintained for up to an hour
if necessary, either to escape
danger or during a hunt.

Long-distance runners
Wolves prefer to trot or lope at about 4 to 6mph and can cover 100 miles in a day in search of food.

Quick thinking

The wolf is very intelligent: its brain is 30 percent
larger than the domestic dog's. Captive wolves learn
after short periods of observation how to undo simple
latches and get to the food rewards behind gates.

Crepuscular canids

The wolf pack is most active at dusk and dawn because it has learned
to operate when humans – its biggest predator – are less active.

THE HUNT

Native Americans have always considered the wolf to be one of the finest and most successful of all hunters, even when it was in direct competition with them for food. Early North American settlers were also in awe of the wolf's strength and power – wolves have been known to track prey for up to 100 miles a day and bring down quarry 10 times their own size. Behavioral studies have revealed what actually happens before, during and after a kill and the high level of collective skill and co-operation involved in hunting as a pack.

TEAM-BUILDING

Much of the wolf's hunting success as a pack is based on careful preparations before the hunt. Individuals constantly revise their skills and practice techniques so that every member is ready to play their part.

The hunter, like the omega, is a specialist animal and is usually female. Females are smaller than the males by approximately 20-25 percent, which usually means they are faster and more agile. There are often one or two wolves within the pack that can sprint like a greyhound – fast enough to catch, turn, or run their quarry into an ambush. The hunter may not always be the alpha female in a large pack because she is too valuable to risk getting injured. She will, however, direct operations from the sidelines and will keep control of the lower-ranking wolves during the hunt. As this is a difficult task, she often initiates a practice session just before the hunt.

First, by adjusting the position of her tail, she excretes an odor which tells the pack which way to turn. She also uses her body to push them either to one side or the other. Second, she lets them know which species is going to be hunted. The alpha female will select the kind of prey most appropriate to the pack's seasonal needs: in winter, often large animals with a high fat content, such as bison, elk, and wild boar, and in summer,

smaller animals such as mountain goats or young deer. She indicates her chosen prey by digging up cached food – such as a piece of hoof – which has been buried for later consumption or for use in training sessions. In summer, food is usually buried around lakes and ponds or along riverbanks where the cool mud just above the waterline acts as a refrigerator.

Having shown the hunters and the rest of the pack which food she wants them to hunt, she must now demonstrate the movements that the prey animal would make while being chased. She usually does this while carrying the food object in her mouth. The alpha male will be allowed to take the food from her and act as if to defend it, showing that he will have control once the kill has been made and the pack begins to feed.

Sometimes a wolf may hunt alone, and it is then more cautious, tending to catch small prey such as rodents, birds, rabbits, and fish.

ON THE SCENT
Wolves have an exceptional sense of smell. Scientists have proved that domestic dogs have a sense of smell ten thousand times more sensitive than our own, and although it has not yet been scientifically calculated, the wolf's sense of smell is far superior to that of the dog. However, it has been suggested that it is one hundred thousand times more sensitive than that of humans. The wolf can detect potential prey, using the wind direction to its advantage, at a distance of nearly $1^3/4$ miles.

Hunt rehearsal
The alpha female (center) uses her body to push and steer the other wolves to the left or right to follow the scent of the prey. In doing this she prepares them for the hunt and asserts her dominance as a decision-maker.

Hunting practice
The alpha female instigates a game of tag in which the young wolves will be shown how to catch and bring down their prey by practicing on each other.

When wolves are tracking the movements of quarry, they can follow the scent of the animal's hoofprints, urine and droppings and can also smell any hair, skin particles or parasites in its tracks. They are also able to smell the tooth decay (from chewed vegetation) of an old animal. Indeed, so honed are the wolf's information-gathering skills that it can tell if the quarry is in poor condition, sick, old or injured and how far ahead it is.

Successful hunting requires various techniques, depending on the size of the quarry. Stalking in long grass or ambush are used to catch smaller animals. During an ambush the pack splits into two or more groups, and one will chase the animal toward the remaining pack members, camouflaged in the trees or bushes. Wolves have been seen to pick up snow in their mouths so that their breath will not be visible to their prey. Once the prey is caught, one bite around the neck and a few shakes will quickly kill the animal.

Another technique is intimidation. Wolves single out their prey and try to get it to run – there is less danger from hooves and horns when the animal moves away from them and cannot turn to defend itself. Wolves have been known to move at a top speed of between 30 and 40 miles per hour, and they can maintain this pace for an hour if they need to. Or, if they are chasing a large, healthy ungulate, such as elk or moose, they can stay the course and deny their quarry food, water, rest and herd security for up to two weeks. The wolves wound their quarry by snapping at it from time to time,

The alpha female will often initiate a practice session

just before the hunt.

and eventually the larger animals will collapse from loss of blood and exhaustion.

TASTE OF SUCCESS

Once the prey has been killed, the pack feeds in an orderly and controlled manner. The alphas do not always feed first but they decide exactly what each wolf is to eat and when. Larger wolves such as the betas need to retain their strength to act as enforcers and will be allowed more food than lower-ranking wolves.

Each wolf is capable of consuming between 5lb and 20lb of meat in one go because it could be several days or even weeks before the pack feeds again. If there is more food than they can eat, wolves have been seen caching the surplus and then marking the spot with urine so that they can locate when food is scarce.

After feeding, the wolf pack relaxes and indulges in play and grooming sessions to ensure that valuable bonds are renewed after the tension and risks of the hunt (wolves make a kill only once in every ten hunts). And then the wolves rest in order to aid digestion. They always remain alert, however, and, if they need to run to escape danger, have been known to regurgitate the contents of their stomachs. Running on a full stomach would not only be uncomfortable and reduce speed, but could cause twisted gut, a potentially fatal condition.

After the hunt and initial feast, the wolf pack often howls to defend its hard-earned meal from other predators. Scavengers such as ravens, eagles, foxes, or coyotes will eventually polish off the leftovers.

By adjusting the position of her tail, the alpha female excretes an odor which tells the pack which way to turn.

Nose to tail
Here the alpha female uses her lifted tail to release a scent and to act as a sign for the other wolves to follow her. She will practice a change of direction when she is some distance ahead of them.

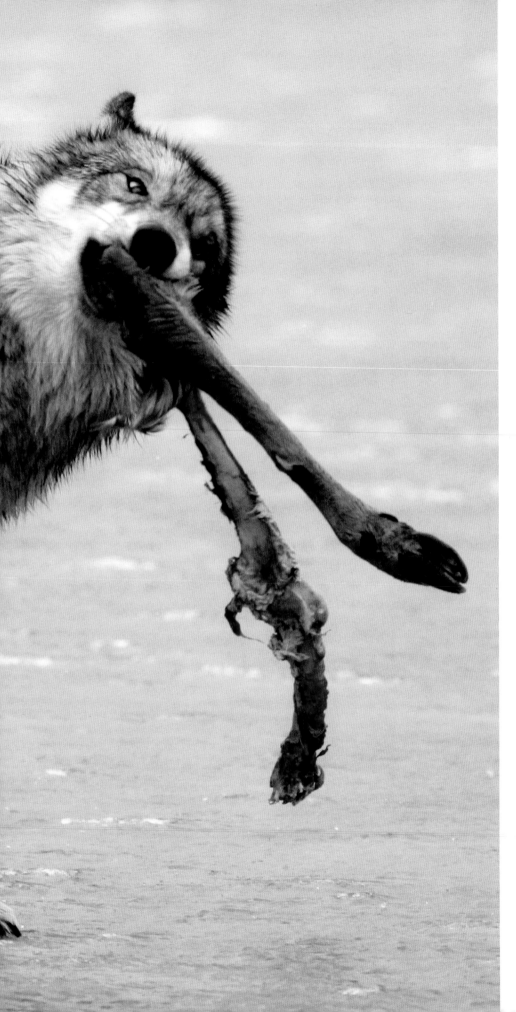

The deer hunters

The alpha female indicates her intention to hunt deer by using a previously cached leg to teach the pack what to look for, and how to catch it. If the wolves approach her from the front, she will demonstrate potential dangers by turning her head from side to side, and by hitting them with the leg to simulate a kick.

Tracking techniques

Wolves find their prey in three ways: by scent, using their fantastic sense of smell; by following tracks; and by chance encounters.

Winning by a nose

The wolf's sense of smell is so sensitive that they have the ability to smell disease and decay in elderly or injured prey from the tracks they leave in the snow.

When wolves are tracking the movements of quarry, they can follow the scent of the animal's hoofprints, urine and droppings and can also smell any hair, skin particles or parasites in its tracks.

Poised for action

This wolf raises himself onto his hind legs as he smells, hears, and finally sees the rest of his pack directing the prey toward him ready for an ambush. This is one of the many techniques used during hunting.

One in ten chance

Wolf packs have a one in ten success rate for catching prey. They compete with both other predators, such as bears and cougars, as well as human hunters.

*The alpha female will select the kind of prey most appropriate
to the pack's seasonal needs: in winter, often large animals with a
high fat content, such as bison, elk, and wild boar.*

Survival of the fittest

Wolves often test ungulate herds for old, weak, or vulnerable individuals. By hunting these animals, wolves keep deer or bison populations healthy because only the fittest animals will go on to breed.

Wolves single out their prey and try to get it to run – there is less danger from hooves and horns when the animal moves away from them and cannot turn to defend itself.

Wolf intimidation
A wolf intimidates a bison to try to make him run. During the hunt, following large prey as it runs away is less risky than confronting it.

Risky business

A kick from a large animal, such as a bison, could be fatal. Male bison often lead and protect their herd and can be very bold and aggressive. They are not easily intimidated by the wolves.

Deflecting danger
The wolf is most at risk of injury when its prey is charging toward it, and so it circles its prey to try to turn the animal away from him.

Staying the pace

The wolf's slender body and long legs are ideally adapted for the tight twists and turns required when hunting. Moving with a fluid motion, wolves also have stamina over long distances.

Closing in

Having chased this bison for many hours, the wolves will finally pull it down by its nose or rump. Once it has fallen, the wolves close in for the kill.

Once the prey is caught, one bite around the neck and

a few shakes will quickly kill the animal.

Flesh, bone and fur

Large, hoofed animals, including deer, make up a high percentage of the prey in the wolf's varied diet. As well as flesh, wolves also consume bone, which provides calcium and phosphorus, and fur to coat the bone to prevent sharp fragments doing any internal damage.

Mobile menu

Herd animals have been known to destroy large areas of vegetation during continuous grazing. The wolf, however, helps to maintain good quality grass by hunting the prey and consequently moving the herds around.

Snowpaws

When traveling long distances in deep snow, wolves will frequently switch places so the animal in the lead does not tire. The slight webbing between the wolf's toes helps it to travel on snow and ice with ease.

Slippery end

During the winter, wolves sometimes chase their prey onto frozen lakes to speed up the kill. Hoofed animals find it difficult to run and stay upright on the ice and will often slip and fall without the wolves having to risk injury by pulling them down.

Snow blocks
Wolves have been seen holding snow in their mouths when close to their prey. This helps them to avoid detection by lowering the temperature in their mouths so that their breath is not visible.

The sound of success

After hunting, the wolves defend both their food and their
territory over long distances by using a low defensive howl.
Increased scenting will also occur to back this up, in and
around the edge of the territory.

Food defence

Ears lowered to the sides, head down and baring of teeth
indicate that a wolf is defending something. Adult wolves teach
the pups to defend their food by stealing it, and then when the
pups approach and try to get it back the adults show their teeth
and growl. The pups soon learn that they must do the same to
keep their food.

Howl of triumph

After a kill has been made, defending territory is just as
important as defending the food. The wolves will howl
periodically throughout the night to advertise their kill
and their intention to defend it.

Cut above the rest

After a kill, the alpha wolves defend their food by baring their teeth and flicking their tongues. These wolves have the right to consume the vital organs such as heart, liver, and kidneys

Sharp warnings

Feeding can appear to be a volatile time, but often the bared teeth and growls are just used to defend a wolf's share of the carcass. The omega wolf is vital in calming such situations and

Smell of success

This older wolf knows from experience the value in hunting and eating particular prey species to increase his scent. His knowledge is respected and used to teach younger members of the pack. Fish is particularly pungent and may be abundant in some wolf territories.

Hunter-gatherer

In times of extreme hardship the wolf will consume fruit,
berries, and nuts to survive. The adult wolves will teach

up to 100 miles a day and bring down quarry

10 times their own size.

Wolf watching

Most wild wolf sightings occur in winter when prey is most active and the pack has to travel further. Generally, wolves will smell humans and hide away long before we catch a glimpse of them.

Light snacks

For many years scientists did not know how wolves survived in areas where large ungulates were in decline. The stomach contents of dead wolves, however, revealed that the animals survived on small prey such as rodents, squirrels and birds when larger prey was scarce.

Sometimes a wolf may hunt alone, and it is then more cautious, tending to catch small prey such as rodents, birds, rabbits, and fish.

Fast food

Though European wolves (above) also hunt and kill prey up to 10 times their own body weight, they regularly eat much smaller animals such as mice and frogs. The wild boar still exists in areas of Europe and is a good source of food for them.

Lone ranger

Packs of wolves can bring down large quarry by co-operative hunting, but the lone wolf must search for small prey, such as rabbits, rodents, and birds, until he or she can join a pack or meet another lone wolf of the opposite gender.

Larger wolves, such as the betas, need to retain their strength to act as enforcers and will be allowed more food than lower-ranking wolves.

Tell-tail signs

Tail posture signifies a wolf's position within the pack and where and when it can feed. Each rank of wolf is allowed to eat certain parts of the prey which will give it the correct scent for its place in the hierarchy.

Meatwinner

This wolf (opposite) may be carrying food back to the safety of her own territory before consuming it. Or she may be returning to feed her pups and the nanny she has left to look after them.

Food storage

Burying food for consumption at a later stage. Often this is done close to water or in a riverbank so that the food is refrigerated and kept fresh until needed.

Eating for others
Because the betas rely on their strength and are often
the largest animals in the pack, they have huge appetites.
They are allowed to consume more food than the other
wolves because they protect the pack.

Bone-breaking bite

The wolf has a bite pressure of 1,500lb per 1 sq in which enables them to bite through and remove the limbs of prey. Many years ago when human limbs were broken and reset in hospitals, 400lb per 1 sq in of pressure was all that was required.

Aid to digestion

Sometimes, like the domestic dog, the wolf eats grass and other vegetation to add fiber to its diet and help with digestion. Low-ranking wolves already have more fiber in their diet because they eat their prey's stomach, which contains digested grass.

Twig toothpicks

When naturalists first saw wolves chewing twigs and branches, they thought they were sharpening their teeth before hunting; it is now thought that they are cleaning their teeth after a feed.

After feeding, the wolf pack relaxes and indulges in play and grooming sessions to ensure that valuable bonds are renewed after the tension and risks of the hunt.

Light relief

Hunting can stretch and test pack relationships. After hunting and feeding, these European wolves enjoy playing together and grooming, which help to establish their bonds with each other again.

Replete

Wolves consume as much meat as they can in one feed – between 5lb and 20lb – because the next meal could be two days or two weeks away. After such a large feed, resting is essential for digestion.

Waking sleep

Wolves have been known to rest for up to 18 hours a day, but they remain constantly alert to their surroundings and can spring into action if predators, prey or rival packs enter their territory.

In the twilight hours
The wolf has adapted its hunting patterns and now prefers to catch its food at dusk and dawn to avoid human conflict.

Night vision
Though poor in comparison to its other senses, the wolf's eyesight is good at night, allowing it to pick up movement in particular.

Queuing for the kill

Scavengers, such as foxes, often live close to wolves and, though
rodents and small mammals naturally form the bulk of their diet,
they also feed on the leftovers from a wolf kill.

Canid competitor

Wolves and coyotes often live close to each other. The wolves will chase and kill coyotes because they see them as competition for food. The name coyote comes from an Aztec word *coyotl*, meaning "barking dog" and describes the calls of these smaller canids.

Rich pickings

Scraps of food left by the wolves are cleaned up by birds of prey, such as eagles. They can often be seen and heard circling above a wolf kill and will come down to feed once the wolves have left the carcass.

Big competition

Bears and wolves often live in the same areas and compete for food. The adults rarely fight but will attack and kill each other's young as they are seen as competition for food. Together with humans, bears are responsible for a large percentage of wolf-pup fatalities. An adult bear can easily chase away any guarding nannies and dig out a den of young pups.

BREEDING

Breeding in North America takes place from January to April. Wolves in the southern regions of their territorial range tend to breed earlier than those in the north because food is available earlier. The Ethiopian wolf, for example, which lives only a few degrees north of the equator, breeds anytime from August through to December.

The female wolf reaches sexual maturity at two years old and comes into oestrus only once a year. There are records in some subspecies of females breeding in their first season, but they are usually too young to be able to cope successfully with pups, and the chances of survival are very poor. Females have been known to continue to produce young up to their tenth year, but this is exceptional as wolves rarely live beyond six or seven years in the wild. Although the alpha female is usually the only animal to breed in a pack, subordinate females sometimes produce multiple litters possibly because significant pack members, such as the alpha female, have been killed, which causes the remaining animals to panic breed to reclaim vacant pack positions or territory.

Scientists are researching whether the type of food the pack eats enables the alpha female to predetermine seven or eight months before her breeding season the number and gender of pups she will have, depending on whether their purpose in life will be to stay with the pack or to move away and establish a new pack in a neighboring territory. Without other wolf packs on the borders of the alpha female's territory, prey is often lost as it escapes into areas where there are no wolves. Wolf packs flush out and drive prey back and forth between territories, so an unoccupied adjacent territory represents potential loss of food.

Adult courtship begins during late winter and early spring, but well before this the alpha female will start to suppress all other potential breeding females by

reminding them of her dominant position in the pack. She does this by constantly wrestling with them and by preventing them from moving in a certain direction by "T-ing," where she blocks their path, thus demonstrating her dominance .

The alpha female also selects nannies who will look after and educate her pups shortly after they have been weaned onto solid food at about four to six weeks, allowing her to get back to her decision-making duties as pack leader. Despite the name, nannies can be of either gender and are selected by the alpha female for their experience and ability to teach pack etiquette to the youngsters. The alpha female employs a complex selection process and initiates play behavior among pack members to determine which wolves are the most balanced and patient and best suited to looking after her pups.

As the female's receptive period approaches, she will increase her suppression of the lower-ranking females to prevent them coming into season at the same time. By growling and snarling and constantly pushing another female around, she can even cause miscarriage.

During mating, the alpha male mounts the female from the rear, and this usually locks them together in a copulatory tie, which happens when a gland in the male's penis swells and the female's vaginal muscles tighten. The tie can last from five to thirty-five minutes; they can even run together for a while if they need to until the tie breaks.

PUPS JOIN THE PACK

The gestation period for wolves is between 60 and 63 days, and birth, from January to April, is usually timed to coincide with the arrival of young prey species to provide the new mother with plentiful food.

For the first four to five weeks of their lives, the wolf pups only have contact with their mother. She suckles them in the den, offering food, security and warmth: the

Peak time
Constant checking of the alpha female's condition is
essential near her receptive time. Courtship behavior
at this time involves a lot of sniffing and licking.

three vital components they need for survival. These components form the basis of all their future education and are either offered as rewards for good behavior or denied to teach them a lesson.

During the first early weeks in the den, the alpha female will start to introduce the scent of other pack members to the pups. When the mother leaves the den she rubs her face and underside around the other adults and nannies to pick up their scent so that the pups will become familiar with them. She will begin to teach the pups, even at this early stage, what type of respect is required for each rank of wolf. For example, if she has the scent of a dominant member on her muzzle, she will take a young pup's head or neck gently in her mouth and turn the pup over to show the submissive position required in greeting this member of the pack.

The higher-ranking pups quickly discover that the middle teats have better quality milk, and they will begin to show early signs of dominance over their litter-mates by maintaining this position when feeding.

When the pups' hearing and sight are more developed at about four to five weeks, the alpha female brings them above ground for the first time to meet the pack and the nannies who will continue their education and care. When weaning takes place, a similar-ranking adult will regurgitate solid food for a pup, helping it identify the correct food for his or her rank. Once the pups have moved onto solid chunks of meat, the nannies often steal food from the pups to teach them how to defend their food.

The young wolf's education involves vital lessons in communication, social interaction and hunting. Young wolves join in with the hunt at about six to seven months, and lessons taught by older, more experienced members of the wolf family are essential for the youngsters' survival and for the successful future of the pack and of the wolf as a species.

The first six to nine months of the young wolf's life are the most crucial. Many do not survive due to starvation, human persecution or loss to other predators such as bears, cougars, or large birds of prey. Sadly, humans are responsible for a large number of pup deaths either directly through shooting, poisoning and trapping or indirectly through logging and general loss of wolf habitat.

Preparing for pups

Getting ready for the arrival of wolf pups often begins seven to eight months before the alpha female comes into season.

Up close and personal

The alpha male remains close to the alpha female during her season. Her scent will change dramatically when she comes into her short receptive period, and he must be the first male to mate with her to ensure his genes are passed on.

Early maturity
Female wolves are usually sexually active during their second year or season; males become active at 22 months. Wolves can breed for their entire life if they stay free from injury.

As the female's receptive period approaches, she will increase her suppression of the lower-ranking females to prevent them coming into season at the same time.

Staying on top

The alpha male and female suppress the other wolves to ensure that they are the only pair to breed, thus keeping strong genes in the pack. The alpha female dominates the other females to prevent them coming into season.

Selection tests
Choosing the right wolves to act as nannies is vitally important. Here an adult wolf is being tested; if selected, it will be responsible for the pups' education from the age of four to five weeks.

Adult courtship begins during late winter and early spring, but well before this the alpha female will start to suppress all other potential breeding females by reminding them of her dominant position in the pack.

Mating season

Wolf mating usually takes place between January and March depending on the species or subspecies of wolf. A tie between the male and the female has to take place to ensure mating is successful. Even though the wolves are quite vulnerable at this time, they can still run together if the need arises.

Paired for life

The strong bond between the alpha pair keeps them safe and healthy, and they will usually stay together for life. If one of them dies or is killed, however, the remaining alpha will select a new mate.

Fleetingly fertile
The alpha female, unlike many domestic dogs, has only one season a year lasting between seven and twenty-one days. The receptive period when mating takes place is even shorter and lasts four to seven days.

Domestic bliss

During courtship the alpha pair spends long periods of time resting together. This pair of European wolves (above) rest together in woodland. The North American pair (left) are joined on the ice by a potential nanny for their future pups.

Waterfront homes
Wolves always live close to water, and the alpha female often digs her den close to a water source, fully aware that she will need to increase her liquid intake during pregnancy and while feeding her pups.

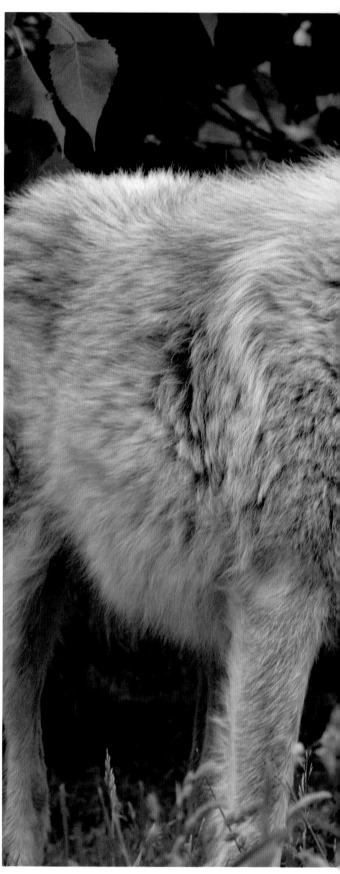

Conserving energy

The gestation period for a wolf is between 60 and 63 days. Toward the end of this period, the alpha female can be seen resting more frequently, saving energy for the weeks to come.

Social climbing

During the alpha female's gestation period, the pack is on its best behavior. Each wolf tries to impress the alpha pair in an attempt to get the job as a nanny.

Infanticide
Rival packs are fiercely territorial, and in an attack pups are seen as future competitors for territory and are usually killed. But some packs have been known to raise orphaned pups in order to boost their own numbers.

Safe haven

The selection of a den site is essential for the survival of the pups, particularly as most of their predators can dig them out. This is why the den is usually positioned under a hard surface, such as a rock, or at the base of a tree to provide extra protection.

Pups as prey

Smaller predators, such as coyotes, pose no threat to adult wolves but would not hesitate in killing a wolf pup or even a whole litter if they found one unguarded.

Adult education
Alphas give refresher lessons
in, for example, balance and
trust, to make sure every wolf
knows how to behave around
the young impressionable
wolf pups.

For the first four to five weeks of their lives, the wolf pups only have contact with their mother. She suckles them in the den, offering food, security and warmth: the three vital components they need for survival.

Blind beginning

Young wolf pups are born both blind and deaf; they find their way to their mother's teats using their sense of smell. At 10-13 days, the pups open their eyes which start blue and later change to golden brown.

Sneak preview

Sometimes the nanny's curiosity gets the better of her and she attempts to take a quick look at her new charges when the alpha female is away from the den. She is taking a risk in doing this because the alpha mother does not tolerate any interaction with her pups until she is ready to hand them over.

Full-time nanny
During the first few weeks spent below ground both the pups and their mother are watched over by a nanny. These animals are totally dedicated to the safety and training of their future charges and won't leave until dismissed by the alpha female.

First outside view

At four to five weeks, the
pups venture to the entrance
to the den. Their development
rate is so fast that in another
two weeks they will be
exploring up to half a mile
away from the den.

The mouth test

The young wolf pup explores its surroundings by tasting

everything and is always on the look out for a potential meal.

The adult wolves will observe and give guidance when required.

Choir practice

The pups listen with interest to the pack howling and will usually attempt to join in with the chorus at three to four weeks. Perfecting the art of howling is essential for a young wolf pup. Usually it's the more dominant pups that howl first, but it's not long before all the pups join in the family howls.

Etiquette lessons

The alpha female introduces her pups to the scent of the other pack members while they are still in their den. She shows them how to respond correctly to the adults depending on their rank.

Early days

For the first four to five weeks
of their lives, the pups only
have contact with their mother.

Semi-solids

When the young wolf pups are weaned, they receive
regurgitated food from the adults after they have fed. This will
be replaced by solid meat as the pups' teeth develop.

Once the pups have moved onto solid chunks of meat, the nannies often steal food from the pups to teach them how to defend their food.

What not to eat
These young pups soon establish a feeding routine based on the right food for each rank. They have been taught how to defend their food using body posture and growls.

Hunting howl

Wolves are active and often howl on the night of a full moon. Rather than calling up the devil, it is more likely that the alpha instigates howling because the moonlight increases the pack's chances of a successful hunt.

237

Defensive techniques

The young wolves learn to
defend their food both at the
kill, with body postures,
growls, and snarls, and, longer
range, by using a deep howl.

The first six to nine months of the young wolf's life are the most crucial. Many do not survive due to starvation, human persecution or loss to other predators such as bears, cougars, or large birds of prey.

Test of strength

Three wolf pups practice their skills in a tug of war. The beta pup has the advantage of strength during this game, but the smaller pups are usually quicker and will often run off with the toy if the beta lets go.

Playing chase

When wolf pups play together, mock hunting is one of their favorite games. Chasing and biting the backs of each other's legs, and running in front of one another are rehearsals for catching prey in the future. Here the nanny is involved in the boisterous play.

Serious play

Constant play-fights help young wolves to learn about pack survival. These sessions teach different hunting techniques, such as the ambush, where some animals hide in the trees and jump out on the other wolves as they approach.

Educational games
Play is used for teaching purposes and to maintain family bonds. Bones or sticks are sometimes picked up and used in chasing games of tag and relay.

CONSERVATION

The gray wolf once had the largest distribution of any mammal, apart from humans, ranging from the Northwest Territories of Canada to Mexico and across much of Eurasia. By the time it was finally protected by the US Endangered Species Act of 1973, it had been wiped out from the lower 48 states except for a few hundred in Minnesota and a few on Isle Royale, Michigan. Similarly, during the nineteenth and twentieth centuries, wolves were exterminated from central and northern European countries.

Governments played a significant part in the decline of the wolf by introducing bounties for dead animals. As early as 600 BC, Greek local government officials paid a bounty of five silver drachmas for each dead male wolf. England introduced wolf bounties in the 1500s, Sweden, in 1647 and Norway, in 1730. The first wolf bounty in North America was issued by the Massachusetts Bay Colony in 1630.

Wolf bounties and legal culls were widespread throughout Europe, Canada and the US. Though culling is an attempt to control wolf numbers, more often than not it has quite the opposite effect, causing what's left of a pack to panic breed.

The gray wolf is now classified as vulnerable by the IUCN (The World Conservation Union) Red List and endangered in the US (lower 48 states) except Minnesota where it is listed as threatened. Despite continued persecution in some countries, such as Russia, the species is now protected by the Endangered Species Act in the US and by the Bern Convention in Europe, which also protects its habitat.

Wolves are now gradually gaining ground in western Europe, with small populations in France, Germany, Norway, Sweden, Finland, Greece, and Italy. There is also now a viable population of about 2,000 Iberian wolves, a gray wolf subspecies, in Spain and Portugal.

Apart from the wolves in Portugal, most of the rest live near highly populated areas in northern Spain, though recent forest fires have destroyed large areas of their natural habitat.

Gray wolves are still found in about 90 percent of their original range in Canada and number between 52,000 and 60,000. In the US, wolf populations have been increasing and there are now about 2,700 wolves in the lower 48 states and between 6,000 and 8,000 in Alaska. Various reintroduction schemes have helped to boost wolf numbers in the US: the red wolf *Canis rufus*, a distinct species which had become extinct in the south-eastern US by 1980, has been returned to parts of its former range and now numbers more than 100; there are now 11 packs of Mexican wolves *Canis lupus baileyi* in New Mexico and Arizona; populations of eastern timber wolves, another gray wolf subspecies, have been augmented in Minnesota and now also roam Michigan and Wisconsin; and there are increasing numbers of gray wolves in the Northern Rocky Mountains, spanning Montana, Idaho and Wyoming. These reintroductions have not been trouble free as some wolves have attacked livestock and have had to be removed by the US Fish and Wildlife Service.

We now know that the alpha female will deliberately produce pups to occupy vacant territories and start new packs in order to cut off the escape route of prey and so increase her own pack's chances of survival. Research shows that it is often the dispersing wolves that are the ones that become a problem to livestock because in seeking vacant territory they sometimes approach farms or ranches.

Dispersing animals also help to prevent inbreeding. In the past, when wolf-pack territories covered several hundred square miles, co-operative pairing of offspring between adjacent packs would create slight but beneficial genetic variation. Now the wolf

often has as little as 30 to 40 square miles of territory, and it is much harder to ensure genetic variety for future generations.

With ever more behavioral studies constantly improving our knowledge about the way wolves live and interact, we are developing a clearer picture of their world and their extreme level of intelligence. Only by

using this knowledge will be able to devise sophisticated techniques to manage the co-existence of wolf and human populations.

Most of our current methods to prevent wolves from taking livestock have been unsuccessful. Simple gate closures can be opened by wolves after only a short period of observation. Electric fencing can be disabled

Fishing wolf

The rapid expansion of towns and farmland diminishes the wolf's habitat and causes a corresponding decrease in its natural prey. So the animal is forced to try alternative food sources, such as fish. Unfortunately, if eaten in excessive amounts, this can dramatically affect a pack's social order.

Yellowstone National Park, where wolves were reintroduced from Canada in 1995, now has 16 packs of wolves.

by snow and guard dogs have been tricked by the wolf's cunning. Wolf packs have been known to send a female wolf forward who will act as if she's in season and whimper to attract the dog. The rest of the pack then appears and kills the animal to get to the livestock.

A guard dog would be a more effective deterrent if it had visual traits such as upright, well-marked ears, a strongly marked muzzle, and a long tail and hackles. Also if the dog were trained to socialize and mingle with the sheep or cattle, the wolf might then regard it as the equivalent of the herd's alpha male.

Ecotourism is a modern phenomenon which raises funds from tourists who wish to observe or photograph wild wolves in their natural habitat. In organizing and running ecologically-supportive holidays, local people can generate a sustainable income by protecting their indigenous wildlife. The positive financial benefits of a tourist-based industry could provide a valuable alternative income for local hunters.

So the wheel of fortune does seem to be turning at last in favor of the wolf, not least in part due to the efforts of numerous organizations worldwide in promoting the survival of this species. Some wolf centers house captive-bred and rescued animals for study and educational purposes, and raise money for conservation and reintroduction schemes.

Yellowstone National Park, where wolves were reintroduced from Canada in 1995, now has 16 packs of wolves, and a positive "wolf-effect" on the whole ecosystem is being noted by scientists. The out-of-control elk population has been halved by the wolves, and this has allowed trees, such as willow and aspen, to regenerate. Beavers have, in turn, been attracted back to the area by a healthy food supply, and wolf kills have pulled in scavengers, such as grizzly bears, ravens and birds of prey. It will be fascinating to see what other effects the wolf, as a predator at the top of the food

chain, will have over time on the park's ecosystem.

The Yellowstone to Yukon Conservation Initiative was launched in 1996 and is an ambitious long-term project which aims to connect wildlife parks and wild areas by conservation corridors all along the Rocky Mountains of Canada and the northern US. It will eventually allow wildlife the space to roam, to interbreed and will create a vast, interconnected mountain ecosystem.

And perhaps one day in the UK, if the Wolf Trust is successful in its campaign for wolves to be reintroduced to Scotland, visitors to the Scottish glens will once more thrill to the call of the wolf.

Losing ground

With the ever-increasing loss of their habitat and continual logging, wolves are sometimes forced to turn their attention to catching cattle or sheep on ranches and open farmland.

Critically endangered

The red wolf *Canis rufus* (above), the world's most endangered canid, was hunted to extinction. In 1980, just before it was declared extinct in the wild, 14 wolves were rounded up by the US Fish and Wildlife Service to be bred in captivity. By the end of 1987 enough animals had been bred to start a reintroduction program, and there are now about 100 red wolves in the wild.

There are now 11 packs of Mexican wolves in New Mexico and Arizona.

European survivors

Wolves prefer to live as far away from humans as possible. But as human populations have increased and as wolf territories and their prey species have decreased, wolves are sometimes forced into European towns and cities to look for food. The territories of European wolves (opposite) are much smaller than North American wolves, and so their pack size also tends to be smaller. European wolves have managed to survive only in the most remote, densely forested or mountainous regions.

Mexican stronghold

The Mexican wolf (*Canis lupus baileyi*) was originally found in the mountainous regions of central Mexico. Now recognized as an endangered species, captive-bred wolves have been released and allowed to disperse into western New Mexico.

253

Worth more alive than dead?

Though a protected species in most European countries, some hunters see no need to stop killing the wolf for sport and will pay large sums of money for the privilege. But with the advent of ecotourism, money can now be generated by people who wish to visit countries to watch wolves, and this has helped to fund conservation work and show local businesses the value of keeping the wolf alive.

Ecotourism is a modern phenomenon which raises funds from tourists who wish to observe or photograph wild wolves in their natural habitat.

Return of the native

The gray wolf (left) became extinct in England in about 1486 and was exterminated in Scotland in 1743. Wolves survived in Ireland until about 1773. The species also vanished from other Western European countries, but now populations can be found in about nine of them.

INDEX